Journey to Ellis Island

Jacket, Design, and Compilation © 1998 The Madison Press Limited
Text © 1998 Carol Bierman
Illustrations © 1998 Laurie McGaw

First published in the United States and Canada by
Hyperion Books for Children
114 Fifth Avenue
New York, New York 10011-5690

This Scholastic edition is only available for distribution through the school market.

3 5 7 9 10 8 6 4 2

The illustrations were painted in watercolor and casein on handmade Japanese paper, Kurotani 89.

Library of Congress Cataloging-in-Publication Data
Bierman, Carol
Journey to Ellis Island : how my father came to America / by Carol Bierman ;
with Barbara Hehner ; illustrated by Laurie McGaw. — 1st ed.
p. cm.
Summary: An account of the ocean voyage and arrival at Ellis Island of eleven-year-old Julius Weinstein who,
along with his mother and younger sister, immigrated from Russia in 1922.
ISBN 0-7868-1411-X (alk. paper)
1. Weinstein, Julius—Juvenile literature. 2. Jewish children—New York (State)—New York—Biography—Juvenile literature.
3. Jews, Russian—New York (State)—New York—Juvenile literature. 4. Immigrants—New York (State)—Juvenile literature.
5. Brooklyn (New York, N.Y.)—Biography—Juvenile literature.
[1. Weinstein, Julius. 2. Jews—New York (State)—New York—Biography. 3. Russian Americans.
4. Immigrants—New York (State) 5. Brooklyn (New York, N.Y.)—Biography.]
I. McGaw, Laurie, ill. II. Title.
E184.J5B549 1998
974.7'1004924—dc21   98-10987 CIP AC

Madison Press Books
40 Madison Avenue
Toronto, Ontario
Canada M5R 2S1

Printed in Hong Kong

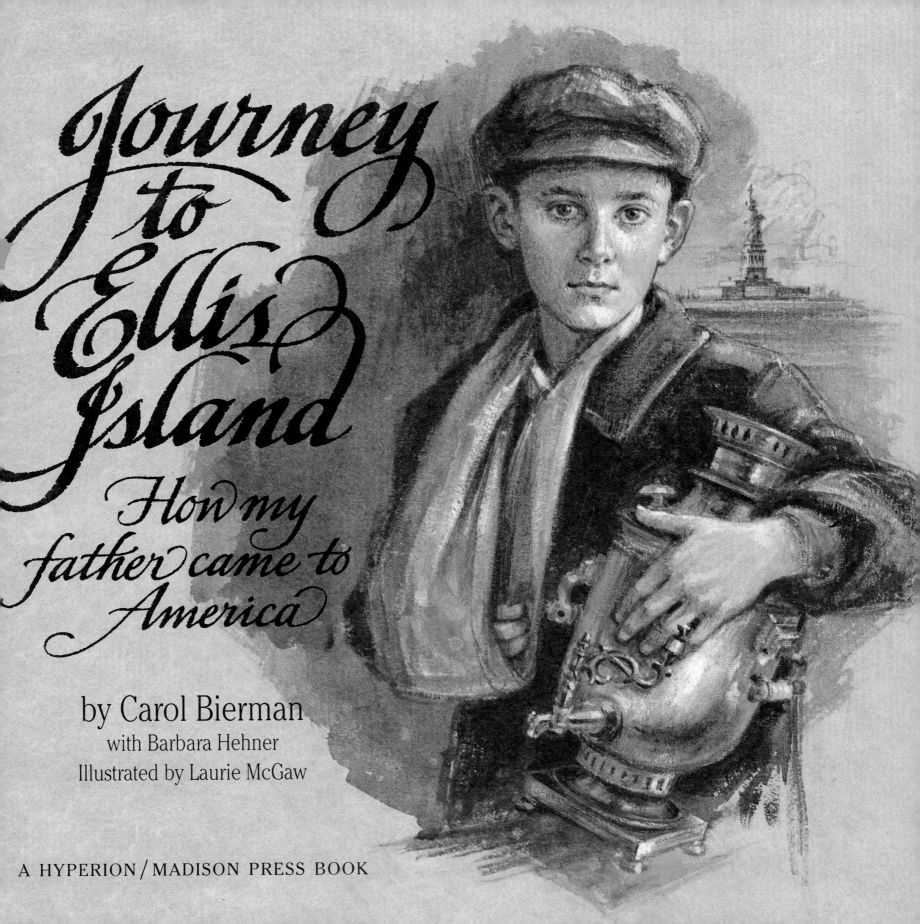

Journey to Ellis Island

How my father came to America

by Carol Bierman

with Barbara Hehner

Illustrated by Laurie McGaw

A HYPERION/MADISON PRESS BOOK

For Julius "Yehuda" Weinstein and all the other children who passed through Ellis Island on their way to a new world.

U. S. IMMIGRATION STATION, ELLIS ISLAND, NEW YORK

KINDERGARTEN

© 1925 D. T. MAGOWAN, MAPLEWOOD, N. J. 13

CHAPTER ONE

Boarding Ship

ROTTERDAM, SEPTEMBER 1922

"Your name, please?" The ship's purser glanced up from his papers at the woman standing before him. He looked very important in his stiff blue uniform.

"Rachel Weinstein. And these are my children, Yehuda and Esther," she answered, pointing at each of them. Eleven-year-old Yehuda craned his neck to see through the crowds of people and piles of belongings on the ship's deck. He shifted the heavy brass samovar in his left arm impatiently. He had never seen such a huge ship before and he could hardly wait to explore it. But his little sister, Esther, who was only seven, clung tightly to her mother's hand. They were finally on the last leg of their journey to America.

Yehuda's mother answered all of the purser's questions, including whether she could read and write.

"Yes, I read and write Yiddish," she answered proudly.

Suddenly the purser focused on Yehuda's right arm, which was wrapped in a sling. "How did your boy lose his finger?" he asked.

The Rotterdam (left) was a large steamship that carried many immigrants from the city of Rotterdam, in Holland, to New York.

Pursers on the deck of the Rotterdam (above) wait to receive first-class passengers. These passengers slept in fancy staterooms with fine furniture and curtains (right). Yehuda and his family had only simple bunks in their third-class cabin (far right).

Rachel gave Yehuda a sharp look and drew him toward her. "He had an accident. It was four years ago. He's fine now," she answered quickly. The purser scribbled busily with his pen and waved them on. Rachel breathed a sigh of relief.

The Weinsteins found their way to a tiny, windowless cabin in the lower decks of the ship. This would be their home for the next nine days as they sailed from Rotterdam to New York.

Yehuda, relieved of carrying the bulky samovar, spent the afternoon running up stairways and exploring the upper decks. Several times he almost got lost, the ship was so large. He even explored the areas of the ship reserved for first-class passengers. Peeking into one stateroom he saw thick carpets and quilted bedspreads. Their own cabin seemed very bare and small by comparison. When Yehuda finally climbed out onto the top deck he saw the ship's lifeboats and gulped in the cool sea air.

Meals were served to third-class passengers in a dining room filled with long wooden tables. Bustling stewards placed platters down the middle of each table and people had to serve

Third-class passengers crowd the deck of a ship bound for America (top). Baggage stickers (above left) were placed on all of the passengers' belongings. The Rotterdam *was equipped with plenty of lifeboats (above) in case of an accident at sea.*

themselves. Dinner that night, and every night afterward, was boiled potatoes and herring. Yehuda hated herring, but he leaned in and spooned up a big plateful of potatoes for himself. Rachel, busy chatting to other passengers, didn't realize that Esther was too small to reach the platters. Her plate was empty and there were tears in her eyes when all the food was gone. "Don't worry," Yehuda said, "I've got enough for both of us." But he was relieved when seconds were served, and he was able to fill up his plate again.

That night, no one could sleep inside the tiny cabin. The rolling of the ship as it moved through the waves made Esther horribly seasick. And once the light was out, they all heard strange rustling and scratching sounds. "Rats!" yelled Yehuda as two brown furry creatures scurried across the cabin floor. Esther shrieked and crawled into bed with her mother. Yehuda curled into a tight ball and covered his head with the blanket.

Over the next few days, Yehuda got to know the ship's crew. They offered to show him the wheelhouse. For a minute, he held the ship's huge wooden wheel and admired the gleaming brass around the compass. It was also a thrill to meet the captain.

Yehuda made friends with some of the other children who were traveling to America in the

Huge ships like the Rotterdam *were navigated from the wheelhouse.*

lower decks of the ship. One little boy asked why his arm was in a sling.

"I lost my finger," Yehuda replied. "The doctor said I shouldn't move my arm, but can you keep a secret?" His new friend nodded vigorously. "Sometimes I take it out of the sling and use it just a little!" They both laughed.

Then the younger boy looked worried. "What if they say you can't come into America? My uncle says that they don't take people who are sick."

"I'm not sick! And my momma will fight for me, she won't let them send me back!" proclaimed Yehuda.

Soon Rachel would be put to the test.

As the huge ship pulled into New York Harbor, Rachel, Yehuda, and Esther quickly gathered their few belongings. Then the family stood at the ship's rail. Looming ahead of them was a giant green statue — a woman holding a flaming torch in the air — and beyond lay the vast city. Sunlight danced off the windows of tall buildings.

So this is America! Yehuda thought to himself.

But Rachel rubbed her palms together nervously. She noticed that inspectors had already arrived on the ship. They were directing most of the third-class passengers onto ferries, but they were turning a few away. She knew that the ferries were bound for Ellis Island where the passengers would be given a medical inspection and questioned before entering the United States. Would they let Yehuda in?

Rachel and the children waited their turn in line. When the inspectors saw Yehuda, they shook their heads. They would not let him board the ferry, and they told the captain that he would have to return the boy to Russia. Rachel began to cry, pulling Yehuda toward her. Esther burst into tears as well.

Yehuda was bewildered. Why couldn't they see how healthy he was? The arm was nothing — it would not stop him from being a good American. Surely his mother would be able to make them change their minds. They had been through too much to be stopped now.

The skyscrapers of New York were an impressive sight to passengers traveling to America on board the Rotterdam *(above). A postcard from the period shows the American flag and the Statue of Liberty welcoming newcomers (left).*

Liberty and Justice For All

CHAPTER TWO

Before the Voyage

RUSSIA 1916

Yehuda could remember what it was like before the war came. Each summer he and his mother, his older sister, Mindl, and his baby sister, Esther, would leave their home in Pinsk for the village of Porusetz. There, his mother was the estate manager for a huge poppy farm.

On long summer days, Yehuda played on the riverbanks with the other children. "Don't go out too far, Yudele!" Mindl would beg when he waded in the river. "Momma said to stay on the bank."

Yehuda had a grown-up

Yehuda, Esther, and their mother posed for this family photograph before they left Russia.

brother who had gone to America before he was born. America was also where Yehuda's father had lived before he had returned home and had been ordered into the Russian army. Yehuda remembered his father scooping him up in his arms. He remembered the scratchy feeling of his father's beard pressed against his face. "You must be a *mentsch* while I'm gone, Yehuda. Take care of your little sister and don't make *tsuris* for Momma and Mindl. When I come back, we'll all go to see your big brother Abe in America."

Yehuda's father never returned. And soon the war came to Porusetz. Yehuda remembered the Russian soldiers arriving first. He had never seen grown men look so dirty and exhausted. The German army was right behind them. They turned their big guns on Porusetz, and thundering explosions shook the village. Mindl was badly wounded. A piece of shrapnel had hit her in the head. Rachel put her in a wagon and drove off after the retreating Russian army, hoping to find a doctor. Just after Rachel crossed the bridge leaving the village, the Germans blew it up.

Yehuda and Esther had been left behind in the care of the mayor of Porusetz. But the shelling from the guns was so heavy that there was no safe place to hide. The mayor told Yehuda to take his sister and follow his mother. Yehuda went down to the river bank and put two-year-old Esther on his back. He had never swum the river before, but he knew that it was shallow and slow-moving. Struggling and splashing, he made it to the other side, with Esther's little arms tight around his neck.

After a long, tiring walk, the two bedraggled children found their mother in the next town. She was mourning for Mindl, who had died from her wounds. Yehuda and Esther cried for their lost sister, while Rachel hugged them fiercely. "From now on, whatever happens, we will never be separated again," she vowed. "No matter how long it takes us, we are going to America."

And so Rachel and the two children set out for their home in Pinsk, where they could pack up their few belongings. But all of Russia was in turmoil and it was hard to find a safe route. Once the family was caught in the middle of a battle, with soldiers shooting all around them. Before they could take cover, a stray bullet hit Yehuda's right hand and tore off the top of his ring finger. A soldier wrapped Yehuda's hand in a bandage. Rachel made him a rough sling out of a long-sleeved shirt, and then they kept moving because it was too dangerous to stop.

Rachel was desperate to get help for her injured son. She decided that, despite the dangers, they must make their way to Kiev, where she had a cousin who was a doctor.

Yehuda's days became a feverish blur. He plodded along, sometimes splashing through mud and snow, and sometimes kicking up dust that made his throat burn. His arm felt like a big, hot drum that pounded out a heavy beat with every step he took. He begged his mother to let him lie down beside the road. But Rachel said, "If you stop, we must all stop. But if you walk, every step takes you closer to the doctor who can make you well again. And when you are strong, we will all go to America." After that, the drum still throbbed through his whole body, but now it was thumping out a beat that carried him onward. "We are GO-ing to A-MER-i-ca. GO-ing to A-MER-ica."

It took them more than a month to reach Kiev. By this time, Yehuda's whole arm was so infected that the doctor thought it should be removed. Rachel begged him, "Please, he's just a little boy. He needs his arm. I know you can save it." So the doctor removed only what was left of the injured finger and cleaned out all the infection. He put the arm in a black rubber cast and a sling, and told Yehuda not to use it.

After that Yehuda's hand began to heal, and the family continued their journey to Pinsk. Yehuda became skilled at using his left arm for everything. It was his job to carry the brass samovar they had managed to bring with them all the way from Porusetz.

But there were other dangers in their path. Within two nights of their arrival

The samovar, a large urn that was used to boil water for making tea, was a prized possession in many Russian families.

in Pinsk, Rachel heard that the *pogromshchiki*, thugs who attacked Jewish people, were coming. Rachel dragged Yehuda and Esther from their beds, and they ran to an abandoned monastery on the edge of the town. They dug frantically in the earth beside the monastery fence until there was enough room to squeeze underneath. Then they hid in the tall grass. Yehuda and Esther were shaking and whimpering with fear. Rachel whispered to them, "It's all right now, we're safe here. The *pogromshchiki* won't find you. Just go to sleep."

Yehuda and Esther were so exhausted that they did sleep. But Rachel stayed awake, and from her hiding place, she could see homes set on fire and helpless people murdered. When Yehuda woke up in the morning, it was quiet. Then he looked at his mother.

"Momma, your hair is all white!" he said in a frightened voice. Indeed, Rachel's hair was now completely white from the shock of what she had seen.

"Yehuda," she said quietly. "Even when we are safe in America, never ask me what I saw here."

The war and its horrors finally came to an end. Rachel, Yehuda, and Esther made their way to relatives in Otvosk, in Poland. There they waited for Abe to send them money for their tickets.

Finally, Yehuda could go to school. But when he came home, his first question was always, "Did we hear from Abe?"

One day, Rachel and Esther greeted him at the door. "Yes! Yes!" Rachel exclaimed, her cheeks flushed with excitement and her eyes sparkling, "The money from Abe arrived today!"

Esther grabbed her brother's good arm and danced around in a circle, singing, "We're going to America. Going to America!"

And so once again the family continued their journey, now toward Rotterdam, in Holland, where they would board a ship bound for the golden land.

CHAPTER THREE

"Please let us stay!"

THE *ROTTERDAM*, SEPTEMBER 1922

Now the last of the ferries carrying passengers to Ellis Island was pulling away from the *Rotterdam*, but the Weinsteins had not been allowed to leave the ship.

Yehuda and Esther had never seen their mother so upset. She had always been the one to calm their fears and comfort them, but now tears streamed down her face. "Please, he's just a little boy, a good boy," she begged the captain. "If they send him back, he will die. There is no one to take care of him there. If he has to go back, we must all go back. Please, help us!"

The captain of the *Rotterdam* could understand why Rachel was so desperate. He had seen it before — people who had made the long journey to America, only to be told they were too sick or weak to stay. He was a kind man who had

This postcard shows the New York skyline as it looked when Yehuda and his family arrived in the harbor aboard the Rotterdam.

New York City and Harbor from Statue of Liberty.

21

taken a liking to this little family. He also knew that his shipping company would have to pay the costs of returning the Weinsteins to Russia if they were not allowed into the country. "Please calm yourself," he said to Rachel. "I will see if something can be done." The captain strode over to the inspectors and spoke earnestly to them.

"Have another look at this young boy. He's not sickly — in fact, he has been all over the ship exploring, while everyone else was

Ferries carried passengers from the ships in which they had crossed the ocean to the Main Building on Ellis Island. Here they were given a medical inspection and questioned before they could enter America.

seasick and stayed below."

The inspectors agreed to let the family go ashore, so that Yehuda could be checked by doctors the next morning. They all boarded a ferry bound for Ellis Island.

Rachel, Yehuda, and Esther were taken to a long building on the far side of the island to spend the night. Inside was a long, narrow room filled with metal beds lined up in two rows. Each bed had a mattress, with a folded blanket and a

U. S. IMMIGRATION STATION, ELLIS ISLAND, NEW YORK

ALIENS ENTERING BUILDINGS FOR EXAMINATION

© 1925 D. T. MAGOWAN, MAPLEWOOD, N. J. 5

U. S. IMMIGRATION STATION, ELLIS

© 1925 D. T. MAGOWAN, MAPLEWOOD, N. J. 12

A crowded ferry approaches Ellis Island (above). Postcards show new arrivals at the Main Building (top right) and an empty dormitory (bottom right). Immigrants had to stay overnight in a dormitory if, like Yehuda, they required a special inspection. Women and children were also sometimes detained here while waiting for a husband, father, or brother to pick them up. Immigrants who were ill were sent to the Ellis Island Hospital.

pillow placed neatly on top of it. "Esther, look at all the pillows!" cried Yehuda with glee.

Rachel perched carefully on the edge of a bed. "Momma," Esther asked in a small voice, "can we have some pillows to sleep with?"

"I'm sure that will be fine," Rachel said, giving her daughter a hug.

Yehuda and Esther ran from bed to bed, gathering their treasure. When Esther had filled her chosen bed with pillows, she plopped down on top and snuggled in blissfully.

Since it was Friday, Rachel began to prepare for the family's first Sabbath in America. She unpacked her precious candlesticks and two *Shabbos* candles. But she couldn't find any matches. She turned to Yehuda, "Please run to those workmen we saw outside and ask them for a match. You must say 'match' in English like your father taught you. Now go."

Yehuda ran off to find the workmen. He stood for a moment, watching them. When one of them looked up, he

Rachel carried these two brass candlesticks all the way from her home in Russia.

yelled, "Match, match!" But what Yehuda said sounded more like, "Metch, metch!"

The men looked at each other and shrugged. "What do you want, kid?" one of them shouted.

Yehuda knew he'd have to try something else. He pretended to hold a match and strike it on his shoe, then he lit an imaginary candle, and blew the match out.

"Matches, the kid wants matches," one of the men said, laughing. The men rummaged in their pockets. Soon they were tossing matches to Yehuda as fast as he could catch them in his good hand. He grinned and bowed to thank them, then ran back to his mother with his prize.

"Look, Momma, I can speak English; the men understood me!"

That evening the children watched as Rachel lit the candles and said the Hebrew blessing. Then she added a few more words in Yiddish. "Dear God, please make them let us stay. We have wandered for so long."

CHAPTER FOUR

Twice Around the Island

ELLIS ISLAND, SEPTEMBER 1922

On Saturday morning, Rachel laid out her children's cleanest clothes. She braided Esther's hair and helped Yehuda button up his shirt. Then they waited nervously for the medical inspection.

It seemed a very long time until a boat arrived, carrying three men in uniforms. One of them could speak a little Yiddish. He explained that they were doctors from the Immigration Service.

The youngest doctor pointed to Yehuda's shirt and motioned for him to take it off. Yehuda was good at unbuttoning his shirt with one hand, but his fingers were shaky this morning. All his ribs showed through his skin. Would the doctors send him back for being too skinny? He stuck out his chest and tried to look as strong as possible.

The doctor used a stethoscope to listen to Yehuda's heart and lungs. Then the other doctors removed the black rubber cast from his arm. They gently moved his arm in different directions, murmuring to each other in English.

A group of young men and boys wait to be examined by a doctor on Ellis Island.

Suddenly the third doctor said, "Can you run around the island?" He pointed to the door and made a circular motion with his hands. The doctor who spoke Yiddish started to explain, but Yehuda had already understood.

"*Ya, ya, ikh ken git loyfen,*" he said excitedly. He knew he was a good runner.

Yehuda bolted out the door and set off on the path that followed the shoreline. As he ran, he gazed out at the gray-green water stretching far into the distance. He could see the statue of the woman with the torch.

He passed the workmen who had given him the matches the day before and waved to them. He rounded the corner, heading toward the vast city across the harbor. Soon he was back, hardly panting at all. Rachel, Esther, and the doctors were waiting for him. Yehuda hoped this was the end of the testing.

Then the young doctor took a rubber ball out of his pocket. He threw it against the wall a couple of times and caught it. He turned to Yehuda. "Can you do that with your right hand?" he asked. Yehuda smiled to show that he understood and reached for the ball.

A postcard (inset) shows what Ellis Island looked like in 1922. The Main Building can be seen on the right, the hospitals stood on the center part of the island, and Yehuda most likely ran around the area shown at bottom left.

U. S. IMMIGRATION STATION, ELLIS ISLAND, NEW YORK

© 1925 D. T. MAGOWAN, MAPLEWOOD, N. J. 2

AEROPLANE VIEW

But Rachel exclaimed, *"Nayn, nayn!"*

The doctors looked confused. The one who spoke some Yiddish tried to explain to Rachel, "We think that his arm needs exercise to make it strong again. We'd like to see how well he can use it."

But Rachel continued to shake her head. Yehuda thought he knew why his mother was refusing. "It's all right, I can do it, Momma — I've been using my arm sometimes," he said. But Rachel took the ball from his hand and thrust it behind her back.

Now the doctors were frowning. The one who had spoken to Rachel before made one last effort. "Momma," he said in a baffled tone, "don't you want your son to stay in America?"

"Ya, ya!" she replied earnestly.

"Then why can't he play ball?" said the doctor.

Rachel's words came out in a rush. "Because it is the Sabbath, and we do not play ball on the Sabbath!" The doctor laughed in relief and explained to the others.

"Well, my friend," said the young doctor. "Do you think you can run around the island one more time?" He made the circling motion with his hands.

Yehuda was off again.

This time he didn't look around, didn't wave to anyone. He kept his eyes on the gravel path and concentrated on not tripping. He pumped his arms

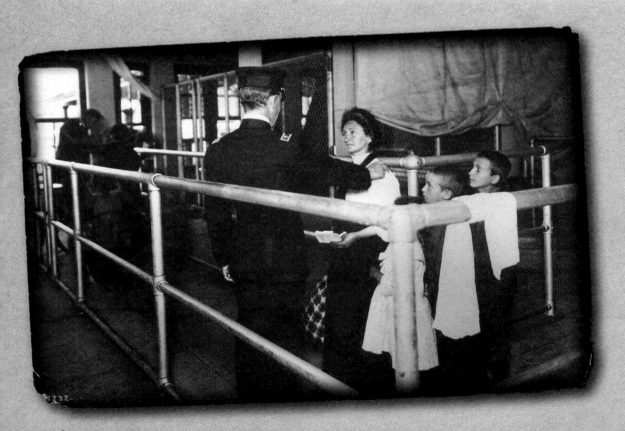

An inspector questions a woman with three young children (left). Most immigrants were free to leave Ellis Island after a brief medical inspection and presentation of their papers. Immigration officials tried to make life pleasant for those who had to stay longer on the island, providing a library, a weekly movie, and even a kindergarten for children (right). But everyone celebrated the day when they could cross over to "the golden land" (far right).

KINDERGART

and lengthened his strides.

Halfway around, Yehuda's heart began to hammer in his chest. The feeling reminded him of running in terror to the river and swimming across with Esther on his back. It reminded him of running to hide at the monastery, and running across the battlefield, and getting shot. It reminded him of his infected arm pounding like a drum: GO-ing to America, GO-ing to America. Well, now he was in America, and he was going to run so fast that they'd have to let him stay here.

He could see everyone waiting for him. Esther was jumping up and down with excitement. The doctors had broad smiles on their faces. Yehuda grinned as he put on a last burst of speed.

"Well, he certainly seems healthy enough to remain in the United States," said the doctor who spoke Yiddish, and the others nodded. He turned to Rachel. "His arm is just weak from lack of use. When it is not the Sabbath, he must play ball. It will not hurt him, it will make him better."

Rachel's face lit up. "Thank you, thank you, I understand," she said. She pulled her children to her and hugged them. "I am so proud of you, Yehuda!"

Rachel was very happy. But she knew that they were not yet free to leave the island.

CHAPTER FIVE

The Final Hurdle

ELLIS ISLAND, SEPTEMBER 1922

Ellis Island, New York City.

The next morning, the Weinsteins were taken to the Main Building on Ellis Island. Yehuda and Esther thought it looked like a castle, with its massive red brick walls edged in white stone and its four tall towers.

"America must really be a rich country if they have such a beautiful building just for people arriving!" Yehuda exclaimed. Rachel nodded, but she was too nervous to answer. They struggled up the staircase to the huge Registry Room with the bags that held everything they owned. Yehuda was still lugging the samovar. He had never been in a room so large.

There were rows and rows of wooden benches crowded with men, women, and children and their bundles of belongings. The hall was hot and stuffy, and it echoed with noise — babies crying, people talking anxiously to each other in many different languages, and officials calling out names. The Weinsteins sat on a bench to wait. Esther curled up against Rachel and soon fell asleep.

Inside the Main Building on Ellis Island (opposite page) was the large Registry Room (above). Here immigrants sat on wooden benches waiting for their names to be called. They would then present their papers before one of the inspectors (left). The inspectors would ask questions such as: What is your name? Where were you born? Where are you going? How much money do you have? Have you ever been in jail? What is your trade? and Do you have a job?

Yehuda saw a man approaching with a big bucket filled with milk and a basket of long yellow fruit. He was stopping at every child, giving each one a cup of milk and one of the strange pieces of fruit. Yehuda watched as one boy bit right into the yellow skin, made a face, and spit it out. Then he saw someone pull the skin down in strips and eat the soft white fruit inside. Yehuda smiled to himself — every day in America he was learning something new!

When the man reached Yehuda, he gave him a banana and one to save for Esther. Yehuda ate his banana hungrily and gulped down the warm milk. But he was still thirsty.

He noticed that the man with the bucket had moved on a few rows and was still giving out milk. Yehuda quietly slipped away from his mother's side and took a seat in a row that the man had not yet reached. When the man came to Yehuda, he hardly glanced up, and the boy got another delicious drink of milk.

Yehuda moved on a few rows to try his luck again. But this time the man looked closely at him. "Hey, wait a minute! Didn't I give you some before?"

Yehuda understood the man's tone of voice and shook his head nervously. *"Nayn,"* he said.

A snack of warm milk and bananas or crackers was offered to women and children on Ellis Island several times a day.

"It was you, all right!" The man wagged his finger at Yehuda. "You can't fool me, son. No more milk for you." Yehuda returned to his mother's side, with the milk-and-banana man's stern eyes watching him all the way.

"Where have you been?" Rachel asked.

"Just wandering around," Yehuda replied sheepishly.

"Stay here," his mother said firmly, pointing to the seat beside her. "We don't know when Abe will come. We don't want to miss him now."

Finally, they heard their name: "WEINSTEIN! Weinstein family, this way, please!" They scrambled to their feet, grabbed their belongings, and hurried after an official-looking man. Then Rachel stopped so suddenly that Yehuda and Esther almost collided with her.

"Avrom," Rachel whispered softly. Yehuda followed his mother's gaze to where a large group of people were waiting behind a barrier. She was staring at a young man who looked very much like she did.

The young man hesitated for a second, and then he yelled, "Momma! Is it really you? Esther, Yudele! I'm your brother, Abe!"

Rachel couldn't speak. She started to cry.

"Momma, don't cry," Abe called. "I'm here to take you home."

The official hurried them on. Abe signaled to Rachel that he would join them. Yehuda looked over his shoulder at Abe as they were hustled away. This was really the brother he had never seen before? He looked so — American!

The Weinsteins were herded into a room where three men sat at a large oak desk behind a wooden railing. Rachel approached the railing, with her head held high and her arms around her children. Another man entered the room and explained to Rachel in Yiddish that this was a Board of Special Inquiry, and that he would interpret for her.

He explained that women were not allowed to leave Ellis Island unless they had an escort such as a husband, father, uncle, or son to take care of them. "My son has come for us — I saw him outside," Rachel replied, turning anxiously toward the door. Just then, Abe was brought in.

The oldest of the men behind the desk looked up from his papers and spoke to Abe. "Are you going to be responsible for this family?"

Abe replied, "This is my mother, my brother, and my sister. I have waited a long time for them to come." His voice was clear and firm. "I am going to take care of them here in America."

The man said, "You need to post a bond in order to take them with you. This means you must leave five hundred dollars with us to prove that they will not become a burden on American society. Do you understand?" Again, the interpreter spoke quickly to Rachel. Yehuda saw Abe's face turn pale.

Abe paused for a moment and then said, "Sir, I do not have five hundred dollars to pay for the bond. But I do have a job, and I was in the

U. S. IMMIGRATION STATION, ELLIS ISLAND, NEW YORK

BOARD OF SPECIAL INQUIRY

© 1925 D. T. MAGOWAN, MAPLEWOOD, N. J. 7

Like the immigrants shown here, the Weinsteins had to appear before a Board of Special Inquiry and prove that they were able to earn a living in America.

American army during the war. I know my responsibility to America, my country, my home." Abe pointed to his family. "I will not let them become a burden on society."

The men studied their papers. They spoke quietly together for a moment. Then the oldest man nodded his head. He looked at Abe sternly and said, "I believe you, young man. You have promised before me that you will take care of your family and that is what you must do." He quickly signed the release order and handed it to Abe.

Abe turned to Rachel and said in Yiddish, "Come, Momma, let's go home to Brooklyn, America!"

Rachel, Yehuda, and Esther were giddy with happiness as they boarded the ferry from Ellis Island to the tip of Manhattan. Yehuda couldn't stop looking at his grown-up brother. Abe looked just as nervous and excited as he was himself. But when Abe looked at his mother, a shadow passed over his face. "How long has her hair been white like that?" he asked Yehuda quietly.

Yehuda started to explain, then he thought about how much there was to tell. They would have plenty of time to talk. "A long time," he whispered back.

Abe sighed. Suddenly his eyes fell on the heavy brass samovar. "Why are you still *schlepping* that thing?" Abe grinned and grabbed it from Yehuda. "You're in America now. We don't need this here." And with that, he threw the samovar overboard.

Yehuda quickly turned to look at his mother — would she be angry? But Rachel started to laugh. Abe quickly held Esther up to the rail to watch the samovar sink, but only a few bubbles marked the spot where it had disappeared.

Yehuda smiled. How many times he had wished he could get rid of that samovar! And now it was gone, just as their old life of running and fear was gone. America is a wonderful place! he thought to himself.

The Golden Land

NEW YORK CITY, SEPTEMBER 1922

Years later, Yehuda remembered his first days in America as a confusing jumble of new experiences. He met his aunt and uncle, who had taken Abe in when he first arrived. Now they made room for three more Weinsteins. Abe was a salesman and had his own car. Yehuda couldn't decide which was more amazing — riding around in comfort on the soft leather seats of Abe's Model T or looking out the windows at the skyscrapers of New York.

Even though Yehuda was twelve years old, he had to start school in the first grade because he couldn't speak English. When his teacher asked him his name, he answered, "Yudel," his family nickname. The teacher wrinkled her nose and said, "Yudel? That's no name for an American boy. We'll call you Julius."

The busy city streets and neighborhoods of New York (above and right) were very different from the world the Weinsteins had come from. The picture (at left) shows Yehuda as a young schoolboy.

From then on, Julius Weinstein was his English name.

Julius learned English very quickly, and within two months he moved up to the second grade. As his language skills improved he skipped from grade to grade. Soon he was in a class with students of his own age.

Rachel, determined not to become a burden on her relatives, found an apartment for her family on the Lower East Side of New York. She opened a small restaurant and also took in boarders to help pay the rent.

By the time Julius reached high school, he realized that his mother needed help to support the family. The school principal helped Julius arrange his schedule so that he could take his most important subjects, including Latin and Spanish, in the mornings. He was then able to work each afternoon. By the time Julius graduated from high school, he could speak eight languages!

Birdseye View of Manhattan, East River
and Brooklyn from Woolworth Building,
New York City.

Copyright 1913 by Irving Underhill, N.Y.

*Like the Weinsteins, many immigrants
from Europe made their homes on the
Lower East Side of New York (facing
page and below) Here, although quarters
were crowded, they could continue to
speak their own languages, buy familiar
foods, and celebrate traditional holidays.
The postcard (left) shows an aerial view of
lower New York.*

A 180

Rachel posed for a formal photograph on Julius's wedding day (left). Years later Rachel's picture was taken with her granddaughter Carol, the author of this book (below).

Even though Julius had to work from an early age, he was always grateful that he had been able to get through Ellis Island. It took a long time before he felt at home in America, but he knew that he would never have to run or hide from anyone again.

Julius attended City College of New York at night while continuing to support Esther and his mother by working during the day. Later he married and had two children, a boy and a girl. Julius and his wife, Marjorie, were married for more than fifty years. Esther also married and had three children. Rachel lived to be eighty-nine years old and was strong and independent to the end of her life.

The Weinstein family quickly adapted to life in the United States. Family photographs show Esther (left) and Julius (middle) looking very fashionable in their youth. When he was twenty-six years old, Julius and his wife, Marjorie, were married. They went to Niagara Falls for their honeymoon (right).

Julius is now in his late eighties and lives in Florida. He is also my father. Several times a year, he visits his children and grandchildren in New York. On the seventy-fifth anniversary of the run that won him entry into America, he returned to Ellis Island with me and visited the museum there. He looked around carefully and then said, "It didn't look like this when I was here, but I still remember it!"

Julius recently visited Ellis Island and sat in the Registry Room (left and below) where he had waited seventy-five years before. Many of the buildings on Ellis Island have been restored (right).

Glossary

immigrant A person who moves to a country that is not his or her native land to live permanently.

mentsch (mench) The Yiddish word for "man." *Mentsch* also means a decent, honorable person.

pogromshchiki (pa-GROM-shi-kee) A term used in Russian and in Yiddish to describe the people who carried out pogroms. A pogrom is the organized killing of a group of helpless people, originally of Jews in Russia.

Sabbath The seventh day of the week observed by Jews from sundown Friday to sundown Saturday as a day of rest and worship.

Shabbos (SHAH-biss) The Yiddish word for "Sabbath."

samovar A large urn with a spigot at its base, used especially in Russia to boil water to make tea.

schlepping (SHLEP-ing) Dragging, carrying, or moving something with difficulty.

shelling Bombarding or attacking with shells. A shell is an explosive charge that is loaded into a big gun and fired.

shrapnel Fragments of a shell, an explosive charge that is fired from a big gun.

tsuris (TSOO-riss) The Yiddish word for "troubles."

Ya, ya, ikh ken git loyfen (Yah, Yah, eekh ken git LOY-fn) Yiddish for "Yes, Yes, I'm a good runner."

Yiddish A language spoken by Jews from central or eastern Europe and their descendants. Yiddish is based on a German dialect with words from Hebrew and several modern languages.

Recommended Further Reading

For young readers:
If Your Name Was Changed at Ellis Island
by Ellen Levine, illustrated by Wayne Parmenter *(Scholastic Inc.)*
• A question and answer book full of fascinating details about immigrants who came to Ellis Island between 1880 and 1914.

For older readers:
Ellis Island — An Illustrated History of the Immigrant Experience
by Ivan Chermayeff, Fred Wasserman, and Mary J. Shapiro *(Macmillan Publishing Company)*
• A comprehensive history of Ellis Island including the stories of many immigrants and beautifully illustrated with hundreds of evocative photographs.

Ellis Island — Gateway to the American Dream
by Pamela Reeves *(Crescent Books)*
• An illustrated history of Ellis Island with special sections on its restoration and how to trace your family history through the island.

Acknowledgments

With love to my husband, Michael, and my children, Beth and Jon, Joshua, and Rena, for their support, and to the memory of my grandmother Rachel, for her tenacity throughout her life. Many thanks to the wonderful staff at Madison Press Books, especially Nan Froman for her guidance and patience and Hugh Brewster for giving a newcomer a chance. Special thanks to Marc and Rochelle Rosenberg for the use of their samovar, to Sheila Fleischer for sharing her candlestick, and to my friend Donna Hulde for being a sounding board. Thanks also to Laurie McGaw for helping to make this story come alive through her beautiful artwork. **— Carol Bierman**

With warm thanks to Sarah Swartz and Ellie Kellman.   **— Barbara Hehner**

Thanks to the wonderful people who posed as models for the book, especially Ryan Cash and Samantha Kohut (Yehuda and Esther) whose *zaydes* Cubby Marcus and Charles Kadin led me to them. Warm thanks also go to Ryan's mother, Deborah Cash, who took the "role" of Rachel, his sister, Melissa Cash, and his father, Paul Cash, who modelled for several characters in the book. Special thanks to Samantha's family — Cheryl Kohut, Gabriel Kohut, and Joseph Kohut — who modelled as well. Thanks also to the following models: Brenda Rosenberg, Jordan Rosenberg, Tori Rosenberg, Jacob Paikin, "Captain" Wayne Watson, Ross Phillips, and Kathleen Phillips. Thanks to Dr. Tom Frater for the use of his samovar, and to Jack Downing and Frank Love for hats. Thanks also to Linda R. Goldman, Ava Wise-Arron, Marcy Abramsky, Bialik Hebrew Day School (Toronto), and the Headwaters Health Care Centre (Orangeville). Finally thanks to my family (my best critics) — Ross, Gwynne, Owen, and Kathleen Phillips — and to Andrea Bocelli for musical inspiration.   **— Laurie McGaw**

Madison Press Books would like to extend special thanks to John Kuss of the New-York Historical Society; Barry Moreno, Librarian at the Ellis Island Immigration Museum; and Jennifer Sylvor, our historical consultant.

Design and Art Direction
Gordon Sibley Design Inc.

Editorial Director
Hugh M. Brewster

Project Editor
Nan Froman

Editorial Assistance
Susan Aihoshi

Production Director
Susan Barrable

Production Co-ordinator
Sandra L. Hall

Color Separation
Colour Technologies

Printing and Binding
Imago Services (HK) Ltd.

Journey to Ellis Island
was produced by Madison Press Books, which is under the direction of Albert E. Cummings.